# The Drought

DANIELLE WALKER

# DEDICATION

I would like to dedicate this book to all the aspiring entrepreneurs.

# CONTENTS

# ACKNOWLEDGMENTS

I would like to acknowledge my Lord and Savior Jesus Christ and also give honor to his father and my father who is our creator 'I AM' (GOD). To those who know me personally I refer to Him as my BOO.

# EUREKA

What did you dream of becoming when you grew up? Can you remember that far back? Did you accomplish that goal? If you did, kudos to you. You made it. You are one of the few out of an infinite number of people who didn't. Now, how many of us didn't become what we started out aspiring to be? ME!!!!! And I'm announcing it with no shame. When I was a kid, my motivation was money. What could make me the most money with the least amount of effort. Remain cute and professional at the same time. I must admit I had a few encouraging voices in my ear that gave me the desire I had of becoming a lawyer. With my dad taking me to some of his clients houses and my grandmothers boyfriend always preaching to me about how important it was to make good decisions to make good money. Becoming a lawyer was the better option for me at least that's what I had assumed. I'm sure all of us have a story to tell on what happened, what could've happened, what should've happened, and what didn't happen that led us to where we are today. But, let's not dwell there.

The objective of this book is to share with you some of the things I've learned and experienced on my journey as an entrepreneur in the beginning leading up to becoming a business owner. My goal is to remain on topic through out the course of this book, but if I end up going left field. I ask that you just roll with me. How does it start is the question that comes to mind. Well, it starts with a 'Eureka'. For those that don't know what Eureka means, it means a cry of joy or satisfaction when one finds or discovers something. To give it a simpler meaning. It's the moment when you get inspired with a new idea that you're passionate about pursuing.

Have you ever daydreamed about creating something that has never been created before and it becoming the best seller throughout the nation and it made you one of the most wealthiest people on the planet. I'm still trying to figure out what it is I can create so I can become one of those people. What's the secret and why hasn't it fallen into one of our laps. The irony of it all is the fact that it has at some point in our lives. However, we don't pursue it. If we do try and make it happen, we tend to share our ideas with someone who don't believe in us and it discourages us from following through. What have you thought of doing that you once were excited about and you told someone and they talked you out of it? Do you remember? Can you see yourself giving it a try now? Why or why not? What's stopping your from having it all? In reality it's you verses you. The only opinion that matters is God's and yours and believe it or not. God is always cheering for you to be the best you that you can be.

My first 'eureka' moment was back in middle school. I was low on cash and I knew my mom wasn't in a position to continue to fill my desire to spend. I wasn't the type to volunteer and watch someone's bad bleep kids and I wasn't the type to volunteer to clean for money. However, I did have a skill I was willing to exploit as long as I was in the mood to be bothered with it. I had the ability to braid hair. Don't get me wrong. Starting out, those plaits looked whack. But, through practice on my uncle, my cousin, my sisters, and myself I was able to perfect it to where someone was willing to pay me. And oh did they. The money started rolling in and I was loving it. I even started braiding elderly peoples hair just to get an extra twenty-five dollars here and there. But the hype didn't last long, because I started out braiding slow. It took me a minute for me to grasp the concept of braiding fast and neat at the same time. Therefore, I would be standing and sweating for hours on end trying to make sure the braids were neat and presentable while I soaked my shirt out. And when that moment came to where I realized I was over worked and under paid. I quit.

There's nothing wrong with trying something and quitting if it doesn't work out the way you anticipated it to. Just be mindful if it's something that you're passionate about, then you may want to go at it with a different approach. Thinking on another 'eureka' moment. In which I've had a few and I'm still in my earlier years of life. There was this one time I had the brightest idea to start my own nail polish line in which I do still own today called 'Drip by Dannie B'. What lead a writer to start a nail polish line is the same motivation that started her on the path to braiding hair. The money was the motive.

Yes people, for those who don't know. I have a nail polish line. I enjoy getting my nails done on my free time. That's kind of like my go to thing to make sure I'm still keeping myself groomed. I may not keep my hair fixed all the time and I may not have the most fashionable fashion. Hell, I may not have the best car out. But there's two things you can always bet you bottom dollar on. Is the fact that Danielle always smells good and Danielle always got some type of polish on those nails. I happened upon the idea one day I was at work and I got bored. I was tired of being there and I got to thinking that I needed to come up with a way to make some more money to help speed up the process of me getting out of there faster. The polish would've been a great idea if I'd already had a following to sell too. As of today my polish is still sitting in a box in my closet. It has potential of becoming everything I envisioned it to be. But the ground work has already been established for when I'm ready to revisit the idea again.

As you can see we tend to have ideas that stick and some ideas we have to let go. But you have to be willing to take the risks. There's nothing wrong with trying and failing. As long as there's still breath in your body continue to strive to fail. One day you'll anticipate failing and strike gold.

# PLAN

A man with no plan is a man that's planning to fail. That goes for women too. I understand the concept of 'winging it'. Believe me I'm very familiar with the statement. I'm the queen of winging things and that's not something that should be boasted about. But there are times when you have to do what you got to do. However, if you can avoid having to do what you got to do without having a brain dump first. Then I highly recommend the brain dump then take action. What's a brain dump? The way that I like to explain a brain dump is when you get a pencil and some paper and you write out all of your ideas on paper in front of you. Once you have everything out that you can think of. You start to come up with your plan on how to move forward with making those things on paper become your reality. You have to make sure to prioritize everything from the easiest task to the hardest and cost efficiency as well. Task lists are ideal in this stage as well. Also, having a planner that you can carry with you daily helps keep you on track and meet deadlines.

Organize, organize, organize. I can't say that enough. And don't pressure yourself if you don't complete a task during the time you set for it to be done. Set realistic goals. I can't recall how many times I've went out on a limb about something I felt passionate about and ended up more frustrated then I was when I first got the idea. I can't recall the number because it's been that many times. You'll come to realize frustration comes when there's no plan of action. I wish I had someone in my corner when I first started out to explain these nuggets to me. Then again, I wouldn't have listened because I felt like I knew it all. But a hard head makes a soft behind.

One thing I'd like for you to take away from this chapter if nothing else. Take having the willingness to remain coachable with you. If you have the ability to remain in an ever learning state and never presenting yourself as the subject matter expert. People will always be willing to help you on your journey and make angel investments into your growth. There is a difference between humbleness and coachable. Only experience can teach you how to differentiate between the two.

Alright there now. Let's say you've got an idea to start a yarn factory and you know nothing about yarn and you know nothing about running a factory. The first thing I want you to get out of your mind is you can't do it because you didn't go to school for it. Who said you can't? And who said you need schooling for it? If you've got the money. Baby, you can do anything you want. But I digress. Now that you've had the 'eureka'. It's time to start planning your dump. This is where you jot down everything you know about yarn. Who needs it, who buys it, how to make it, when is it in season, and the cost of goods. This is just the basics of what you know personally. And then you go and start researching all of the fill in details of what you don't know and what you thought you knew but you were wrong.

I can almost assure you once you've reached this point in your research that your mind has changed several times over. Either you're going to say to hell with this yarn factory or you're going to make a decision to just be a supplier rather than to dig too deep into becoming a manufacturer.

Remember, you haven't even begun the research for what's needed to run a factory or considered the overhead cost. (Gee-wiz) But you just may be that one. It ain't for everybody.

Now that the dump has been established. You have to start writing out your plan. What items you are going to tackle first? Again, don't overwhelm yourself. Progress in any form whether small or grand, it's still a push towards making your dream reality. Start with a list of five to-do's for the month. I understand your eagerness to make things happen, but you also have to leave room for the unexpected road blocks. And there will be road blocks. After you've jotted down those five, start considering what's going to be required of you to complete those tasks individually. Nothing is ever a one and done. There's always an additional unexpected step required on the road to checking one of those items off the list. So if patience isn't your best friend. Then, I encourage you to start becoming familiar with those traits.

Plan your crash. What do I mean by this? I mean you have to schedule a date on your calendar where you do nothing entrepreneurial related. You have the right to work yourself to the bone all the way up till this date. The goal is to over work yourself until you can't take it no more and then enjoy the reward known as 'rest'. Once you start this journey I want to make sure I make it clear that there is no turning back. If you happen to be one of the determined ones that come few and far between. Then, you will never rest until the job is completed and then not even then. There is going to be something in you that won't allow you to stop even when you pray to have the ability to stop. So plan your crash and see your task list through.

Prepare your family for the ride. There are going to be times where you are going to be considered a A-hole. And that's okay because it comes and goes. When your back is against the wall and it feels as though everything you've tried isn't working, don't take your anger out on your family. Prepare them for what you are about to embark on because they didn't ask for this. Also, prepare yourself to become a slave to the creativity. The closer you get to finishing the more you are going to crave more. It can become life consuming if you're not careful.

If someone would've told me the boredom that sparked me to write my first novel would've been the cause of an itch I could never satisfy. I would've never picked up that pen. I don't regret any of the choices I've made. I just wish I was better prepared for the journey or at least informed. But we can't argue with destiny right. If it's meant for you, your passion is going to drive you.

Plan to miss events, birthdays, and forfeit a countless amount of trips. You no longer have that luxury. You are a business owner now. All of your excess funds outside of your living expenses are no longer considered excess. We'll talk money later. I want you to fully understand your life and your freedom is over in a way. It's like a second marriage. You are truly married to your vision and the way you treat it is the way it's going to treat you. You give and it gives. You get what you put into it. If you half step then it shows because you won't have anything to show for the time you can't get back. So plan your days as if you're working with something delicate because you are.

# BUDGET

What do you know about budgeting? Is that word foreign to you or are you familiar? Do you have a budget that you live on now? If you're not living on a budget, start now. A budget is an estimate of income and expenditures for a set period of time. Typically when we think of a budget, we think of something short lived. However, when it comes to running a business. Every decision you make is centered around a budget. You can't make a purchase without a budget. You can't schedule a meeting without a budget. You can't even promote your material without a budget. Let's explore budgeting a bit more.

When I first started pursuing my goal of publishing my first book *The Ultimate Betrayal.* I didn't have a budget. Honestly, I knew nothing about publishing a book or formatting. I was working as a security officer making nine dollars an hour, for forty hours a week. That was good money to a twenty-two year old with no real responsibilities. The moment I assumed I was done with the first draft, I knew I needed a editor. So I googled and asked several social media friends if they knew anyone that could assist. To my surprise a editor costed way more than I could afford at that time. And when I thought to go the self-publishing route when none of the publishing companies I'd submitted to accepted my manuscript without a literary agent. I soon learned I couldn't afford the self-publishing option either. They wanted thousands of dollars of which I didn't possess to have my story told. And I cried. Please know that there is nothing wrong with crying when things don't go you way. Sometimes you have to just let it flow. And don't allow anyone to make you feel any other way.

Eventually, the Lord placed people in my life that assisted me with getting the job done. However, He went about it in a different way. Sometimes your plan isn't what God intended for you and you have to be open for change. Even though I couldn't afford to use someone else's services to make my dream come true. I could afford to start my own publishing company and publish my own work. At my own pace and on my own terms.

Another incidents I would like to share is when I found myself trying to manage one of my friends music careers. Yes, I was once invested in the music industry. There came a time when my artist wanted to shoot a video for song one his songs and it was my job to go out and assist with securing someone to do the filming. Low and behold us not having a budget put a strain on our progress. Why? Because we would have to revisit attempting to film once we've saved up the money to afford that service.

Not having a budget can slow down your momentum. Think about it this way and I'm going to give you a scenario to prove my point. When I launched my first book, I promoted it as if my life depended on it. I expected everyone to go online to purchase the book and have it mailed to them directly. What I didn't count on was everyone wanting to purchase a hardcopy from me and have me sign it on the spot. I assumed because I couldn't afford the hardcopies myself at that time that it would be understood by the consumer to purchase via web. I lost a lot of money because of that assumption and by the time I was finally able to afford hard copies. I lost the momentum of the desire for the book. Have your shit together.

Another nugget I would like to share about budgeting is to know the costs of services rendered in advance. What does this mean? This means you need to know in advance how much someone charge for their service before you do business with them. Why is this important? So you won't get taken advantage of. I'm sorry to have to break this to you. Everyone ain't you and everyone ain't honest. There are people out here that will use your eagerness to move the needle forward to make you a victim of fraud. The day you decided to step outside the box and follow your dreams. Is the day you signed up to become a victim and have welcomed scammers in your life. I know it sounds farfetched, but don't take my wisdom for granted.

When you don't have a budget you are allowing the servicer to charge you whatever they want for their services. Especially if you didn't ask them the cost of their services in the beginning. Also, beware of those who ask you for your budget amount. They are doing this so they can counter you and say that they can do the work for that same amount. This is why it's important to ask for their service fee list. If they can't provide you with a list, then this is not the person you want to do business with. Your goal is to get as much work done without having to compromise quality at a sensible rate.

Another hot topic I would like to throw in here just for the sake of making you aware. Be sure to make room for an accountant. If you decide to opt out of hiring an accountant, download a budgeting application. Accountants are important to the growth of your business. Their job is to focus on saving you money and ways that you can get the best value from your dollar. As of today, I do not have an accountant. However, I have one that I've had my eye on and am making the necessary adjustments within my lifestyle to afford her. I can share this information with you, because

I've come to realize the importance of having one. But I recognize what's important to me now, may not be important to you in the beginning phases of starting your business. P.S. To save yourself from heartache later. Please go ahead and invest in a part-time accountant.

# MARKETING

It's not what you think. Marketing is the bread and butter of your business outside of customer service. If you don't have a solid marketing plan, prepare to flop. You can't make money if no one knows about you. You can't make money if whatever you're pitching isn't appealing to the consumers eye. You can't make real money until you have a marketing company that specializes specifically in marketing there to promote your brand.

When you think about marketing what's the first thing that comes to mind. When I first started out I assumed marketing meant posting my product online and people would buy it, because I promoted it every day. Boy was I in for a rude awakening. I didn't get a real glimpse of what it meant to market your product until I started working with Janari (J-dro). Janari at that time was my best friend and he was a music artist. He was a triple threat. What is a triple threat in the music industry you ask. A triple threat in my opinion is someone who writes their own music, produces, and performs their work. When I first started following Janari around. I was exposed to the business side of the industry. I assisted with setting up photo shoots, hands on with the creation of the album covers, and made sure some of the Dj's would play our music. All of these things are important and are apart of the marketing process for an artist and or any other product you may have.

You can never have enough money, but there is a such thing as not having enough. There's a saying 'it takes money to make money' and I never knew how true it was until I tried to start making my own. The difference between me and Janari over the years was the fact that he had the money to fund his projects, whereas I didn't. Unfortunately, we both still ended up in the same place. Which means we both weren't as successful as we'd both had hope to have been. The key that I've learned that we both were missing was a publicist.

A publicist is the person that's responsible for publicizing a product. They take your story and make it interesting. They're the ones that make sure you get those interviews and product placements in stores and magazines. They create the buzz for you. It took me five years to recognize the importance of having one and how they are truly the makers of your career. They have all of the contacts you don't. They've built those relationships you haven't. They are the door keepers and you have to have money to play. I was fortunate enough to find a publicist that I would love to place my career in her hands. However, as of right now. I still don't have the funds to afford her services. Yes, I can take out a business loan to cover the expenses. But, how much would truly be enough.

Beware of the marketing trolls on social media that try to convince you of guaranteed sales with the help of their services. We are living in the age of scammers and they are relentless. Receipt checking is extremely important. You need proof of success. Don't become a victim when you don't have to be. Do things that will appeal to you and catch your attention if you were the consumer. If the thing you are trying to promote isn't appealing enough for you to purchase then no one else will.

# DOUBT

Nothing will sabotage your success more than doubt. Doubting your ability to succeed in one of the most vulnerable times in your life is one of the biggest mistakes you can ever make. I know it's easier said than done, but you had faith enough to start. Why not have courage enough to see it through. There's going to be a lot of obstacles you're going to have to overcome. But you can't give up when the road gets tough. There were many times I myself threw in the towel, because I couldn't see a way out. But there was always something in me to push me into pressing forward. I can honestly admit that most of my work was sparked from boredom. As though I have nothing else to do, so why not work. Even when I want to be done completely and just be normal. It never happens because I just can't give up.

Thus far, I've been blessed to be able to say that I have five books published and am working on this one and I have another one I've started as well. But because of my frustration of the others not being as successful as I'd like them to have been, because it's purely good writing. I've allowed that doubt and unhappiness to take over my desire to keep moving forward. But here I am still working right. What I've come to accept is it's just not my time yet. Who knows what success would have done to me as a person if I'd received it prematurely. I honestly believe you have to be mentally, spiritually, and emotionally ready for fame. Especially if you're trying to live a life that's pleasing unto the LORD. My life's desire is to please God and do everything I can to remain in His good graces to make it in to heaven when the time comes. Therefore, HE knows that if I'd receive the financial success without fully being ready it could potentially hinder the relationship we have. And I don't ever want that to happen. Nothing is worth your relationship with God, nothing.

I had this personal trainer once that believed in me and what I was trying to achieve. He became a good friend of mine until things got awkward when I thought I was romantically attracted to him. I realized I didn't but it was kind of to late because I had spoke on it. But I digress. He would encourage me to watch motivational videos to try and get me to shift the way I was thinking. I think he could sense my defeat and was trying to encourage me to keep going. It's hard to see the light at the end of the tunnel when finances is your biggest obstacle. Even though I am grateful for my home and all of the adult responsibilities the Lord has blessed me to be able to afford. Because of this big responsibility I haven't had the financial freedom I was so accustom to. But, I can't blame it all on my mortgage or car note.

You have to take responsibility for the things that you've done to hinder your growth. One thing I've learned about myself is when there's no debt. I create it. I blame it on the poverty mentality that I'm trying to break. That need to always spend even when you don't have it to spend. But the bills stay paid. If you make wise decisions financially to remain debt free. Then you'd have the funds necessary to fund your dream. I'm blessed to have two dads and one of them always say 'doubt your doubts, doubt your fears, but don't doubt God'. Believe that God didn't gift you your talent for no reason. Therefore you have to keep working until He says it's time for you to rise to the next level. There are people waiting on you to get to where you're supposed to be. Some you know and some you haven't met yet. Therefore, giving up is not an option for you. Trust if the Lord see you getting to comfortable where you are and you're not doing what He has planned out for you to be doing. He's going to stir the pot or shake up your situation to force you to do what it is He wants you to do. Using myself as an example: anytime I find myself in a place where I'm not writing or being productive and get comfortable with the way things are. Something happens that places me in a position to where I can potentially lose my job. And in those moments I snap out of whatever whole I've found myself sunken in and I get back to working on my book at the time.

You don't ever want to get to a place where the Lord has to step in and make you move. It's not a good feeling. Yes it means He cares for you and wants you to succeed, but that push will freak you out and make you feel as though your whole life is over. Doubt is an attack from the enemy to get you to stop doing what he knows will have an affect on other peoples life that can lead them to the Lord through Christ. Especially if you have a calling on your life in ministry. Most ministers are attacked in their minds and in their esteem. You have to stay focus. You have to stay prayed up and you have to stay in your word. That's the only way you're going to get through this attack.

Fear is an unpleasant emotion caused by the belief that someone or something is dangerous. Knowing this why do you fear succeeding. I've always had an issue with the unknown. Not knowing when or what's next has always bothered me. But those are the risks we take when we try and make our dreams come true. My brother is an amazing baker. My great grandmother taught him how to bake cakes and he took what she'd shown him and made it his own. Even though I've been in business longer than he has. He has been more successful than I financially, because he provides a product that's in demand. Yes, there are other bakers out there that do exactly what he does. But, their product doesn't come close to the way his cakes taste. I'm sharing this story about my brother with you because I want to show you something. A few years back there was a restaurant looking for someone to provide them with cakes. They were going to pay for the service and it also could have opened up other avenues for my brother to make even more money. I tried to encourage him to take the opportunity because I saw how it could benefit him and it could change his life for the better. He didn't take it and I believe it was because of fear. I never asked him if he regrets not taking the offer. But I do believe he thinks about it sometime. Realistically I believe he made the best decision for himself at the time, because if the business got to big. He'd risk having to share his recipes with other people and risk the quality of his cakes.

If you've sacrificed time and invested a dollar or more into whatever dream you're chasing. If it make sense to you, keep going. At least make an effort to say you gave it your best shot. But don't allow doubt or fear to stop you from trying. You don't ever want to get to a place where you have regrets that you never did. 'Doubt your doubts, doubt your fears, but don't doubt GOD.' -Bishop Leroyal Monte Cole

# MOTIVATION

What are you doing it for. Who are you doing it for. What's the driving factor behind why you want your product or service to succeed. Are you doing it for family. Are you doing it to prove that you can. Is it for self-gratification. Is it for fame. Is it for the fortune. Is it for your pride or self-esteem. Are you doing it because you feel you have no other choice. Are you doing it for time freedom. Are you doing it to flex in front of your peers. Are you doing it to change the world. Are you doing it to become a positive influence to those coming up behind you. Are you doing it just to say that you are the first of your family to ever do it. What's your motivation? These are the questions you really need to ask yourself. You need to figure out what's the driving force that keeps the fire burning in you to continue to pursue your dream. If you don't figure this out during the early stages of your pursuit. It's going to be easy for you to get distracted and content.

My motivation is steamed from my desire to no longer have to answer to another individual. I have a problem with the thought of one person having the ability to decide if I'm going to be able to sustain my livelihood contingent on if I do what they say or not. Every time I think about having to sit in the office with my supervisor over something I've done wrong or if a customer is not satisfied with the level of customer service I provided. I cringe. It's the most demeaning feeling in the world to me to have to explain my actions to another adult. I'm not a child, so don't treat me as such. And I have to find a way to break free. Being your own boss doesn't mean you're not going to have to please your customers. However, the way you go about doing so is totally up to you.

What would you lose if you gave up on chasing your dream. Personally, If I threw in the towel and gave up on writing. I'll be risking the possibility of ever being recognized as a pioneer in the art. I'd also forfeit my desire of ever filming my first motion picture. We all have something to say and many have taken steps to assure themselves that they're being heard. Whether they chose to write it, film it, or speak it. The message was relayed. I want to leave something for my children. I want them to be able to say that their mom was a writer. I want my grandkids and my great grandkids to be proud of me. I want my work ethic to teach them that they can do or become whatever they want. Nothing great happens overnight and God can't bless a thing you haven't put effort into for Him to bless. You have to do the work. Use this time to think of things that motivates you to keep the fire burning.

# INHALE

Breathe in. Take a moment to take it all in. Take in all of the positivity. All of the positives around you succeeding. All the accolades. All of the people that's going to cheer you on during your struggle and after your struggle. All the money you have the potential to make. All of the lives that will be impacted in a positive way. All the people you're going to help. All the people you're going to inspire. How you're going to change your parents lives for the better. How your life is going to change for the better. How many jobs you may create for others and how many up and coming individuals in your same field you're going to reach once your reach is expanded.

Now think of all the negatives. Think of all the long nights you've stayed up or will stay up without sleep. Think of all the anxiety attacks and panic attacks you've had and are going to have. Think of all the people that are going to try and talk you out of doing what you desperately want to do. Think of all the family gatherings you're going to miss. Think of all the gatherings you're going to miss with your friends. Think of all of the time you wont be able to get back from you investing it into your dreams. Think of all the money you've invested. Think of all the scammers that scammed you into thinking they were going to do a good work for you only for you to end up more frustrated and in search for someone else to do the job. Think of all the days you cried and prayed and pleaded with the Lord to help you. Think of all the relationships you've lost due to unsupportive individuals. Think of the days you felt alone and the days to come when you're going to feel that way again.

Think of all the weight you've gained from eating your feelings. Think of all the weight you've lost due to stress. Think of the blood pressure medication you were prescribed due to all of the voluntary stress you put yourself through. Think of all the missed selfcare appointments you've forfeited for the cause. Embrace it all.

# EXHALE

Now, breathe out. Let it all go. Everything you were harboring that was holding you back. Everything we listed in the previous chapter, lay it all out and let it go. You've named the issues. You've named your fears. You've named your doubts. Now it's time to let it go. You are the only person standing in your way. If you don't make it to the height of your desired career. It's because you blocked you. No one can stand in the way of you achieving whatever it is that you want to achieve. And, if they are. That's because the route you're trying to take isn't the route the Lord has set out for you. There are no short cuts to the finish line. You have to run the race fair and square. Any shortcuts you try to take will come back and bite you in the long run. You don't want to have endured the hard times just to gain everything and lose it once acquired because of something you did in an dishonest manor.

You deserve to go through this test with ease. What can you do to make this process less stressful for yourself. The easiest thing for us to say is to try and remain positive. It's even easy for us to say to continue to pray about it. Honestly, those things are good choices and I won't lie to you and tell you that they don't work. But what I can say is those things are easily said than done. You may hear that statement a lot because it's true. It's very easy to say what to do before you're faced with a situation when you don't feel like praying, or you don't have anything positive to think about. My only advise when you're facing those situations is to go through it and take it one day at a time. Breathe and focus on the today. Tomorrow will take care of itself.

# LAUNCH

It's launch day. You've done it. Everything is complete. Press 'launch' and pass 'go'. If you don't take anything away from the information I've shared with you thus far. Take 'launch' no matter how imperfect you think your product is with you. Your audience don't know the difference between right and wrong. They don't know your graphic designer messed up on the color scheme. They don't know the manufacture issued out defected lids. They don't know the pronunciation of your title is incorrect unless you point it out. To them this is how it's supposed to be. To them it's perfect. To them it's worth purchasing. You're the only one stressing over the little unnoticeable things. So what if they criticize it. At least you have something to criticize. Their criticism offers you an opportunity to make those corrections on the next release. The world isn't coming to an end because you've made a mistake. So let go and let God.

Let's go over a few pros that comes with launching. Recouping the money you've invested. Making a profit off of your product after all of your expenses have been recouped. Gratification, relief, and accomplishment. Just to name a few. These are benefits of releasing your baby to the world. Self-esteem boost, something to be proud of, another reason to make your mama proud and happy she had you. I mean what do we really do it for if not to make our moms proud. My mom and I don't have a lot of things in common. But I enjoy hearing her tell me she's proud of me when I achieve something I worked hard to achieve. It's the second greatest thing she can ever say to me next to telling me she loves me. You deserve to promote and sell your gift. You've earned the right to. You've sacrificed so much to get to this point. Why not go ahead and cross the finish line.

# LIVE

Life is a gift that we all take for granted at times. I want to encourage you not to get to wrapped up in your project that you forget to enjoy the life God blessed you with. You have to try and find a balance. It's important to try and make time for family, friends, and personal care. It took years for me to grasp this concept because I thought the most important thing at that time was my work. But, I've found creating memories and building relationships are. You can make time to work on whatever it is you're working on, but you can't make up for lost time with the ones dearest to you. I still haven't mastered the art of balancing without one end suffering. But I have made progress in finding time to be present for them both.

Make an effort to explore. I know traveling isn't ideal right now due to Covid-19, but we'd be able to move around at some point. I don't want you to miss out on trying and experiencing new things because of your focus. You won't be young forever neither will your peers. Go to that family bar-b-que. Go to your friends baby showers and weddings, because those are the moments you remember when you're old. You want to have stories to share with your kids and your grandkids. The best advice comes from experience. It's hard to take advice from someone who's never experienced the thing they're trying to council another about. Don't waste time and don't let anyone force you to do things you don't want to do. Wake grateful and go the sleep thankful. Know I love you and I wish you success in all of your endeavors. Smooches, Danielle.

# ABOUT THE AUTHOR

From the author that brought you 'The Ultimate Betrayal, The Next Door Neighbor, Hazel Eyes, Watch This, and Walk with Me'. Danielle Walker continues to share her experiences with her audience in this motivational in hopes to inspire them to keep going. No matter the obstacle, she continued to strive past them and put one foot in front of the other. Doubt your doubts, doubt your fears, but don't doubt GOD.

www.ingramcontent.com/pod-product-compliance
Lightning Source LLC
Chambersburg PA
CBHW032021190326
41520CB00007B/574